THE ODD SIDE OF LIFE

Thoughts in Prose and Poetry

ANN SEARS

ISBN 979-8-89309-281-3 (Paperback)
ISBN 979-8-89309-282-0 (Digital)

Covenant Books
11661 Hwy 707
Murrells Inlet, SC 29576
www.covenantbooks.com

Dedicated to the love of my life, my husband, Sam, who always believed in me and supported me in all my endeavors.

INTRODUCTION

"Poetry is dead," my dear friends all said.
We'd rather read a story—
but nothing too gory!
Who wants to read verse written in rhyme
When we have such precious reading time?
"I do," said a voice so meek. "I
do," the voice began to speak.
"I want to read verse written in rhyme—
Of lovers and loss, of death—the divine!"
"Who is that voice?" I asked
aloud—to find only
ME alone in the crowd!

Since I was a child, listening to my mom read
nursery rhymes and to the lovestruck poetry
of my teen years, I have always loved the way
a poem could express such profound feelings
in a few words or sentences. Even though

poetry is probably one of the last books most people choose to read, I hope that because you have picked this particular book, you will find pleasure in the words I have written.

ON AGING

No, no, *no*, I am not old! For you
to suggest it is much too bold!
Where are the wrinkles and
graying hair? And when do you
find me in my rocking chair?
I'm young and gay and dancing
each night. To suggest that I'm
not just gives me a fright!
But then I awake and realize it's all been
a dream. I look in the mirror, and
I'm ready to scream! Who is that wrinkled
old woman glaring back at me?
Goodness! Gracious! It's me I see!

I guess, if we try to keep our sense of humor, this aging business wouldn't be quite so dramatic.

Life is an effort as each day passes by.
I wake up each morning
with such a deep sigh.
My bones are all creaky—ankles,
knees, legs, and hands.
It's amazing how much pain
this ole body can stand.
TV is boring; most of my friends are dead.
I looked at the paper but forgot what I read!
My eyesight is failing; my
hearing's going too.
You'd think, with these challenges,
I'd feel oh so blue!
"Stop your complaining," I say to myself.
"Each day that you wake up
is loaded with wealth."
Birds are all singing; flowers
continue to bloom.
I have enough blessings to fill up a room.
My life has been long and
filled with good things,
And someday I'll hear heaven's
angels as they sing.
But for now, I'm so grateful
another day's gonna come;

I'll enjoy each one fully till I'm
called heav'nward home.

As much as it pains me to think that
I am aging, I look at the challenges facing
our youth today. Modern technology has
completely changed the way we relate to each
other and the way we learn and grow. Maybe
I am content to be the age I am and can plead
ignorant of some of the new high-tech doo-
dads and ways of communicating.

Would you really want to relive your youth?
Tell me now, and tell me the truth!
Do you want to have those gangly limbs and
Nasty zits on forehead and chin?
Do you want to wait for your phone to ring
Because you and that cute guy
could have such a fling?
I don't think so because I now know,
There's no better time than
the time I'm in now!

When I was young, things were so much
simpler. We had wild imaginations to keep our-
selves amused, instead of playing video games.

We would ride like the wind,
my stick horse and I—
Across a wide prairie, under
a blue western sky.
Sometimes I was the bad guy—
sometimes I was good.
It made no difference to my
horse made of wood.
With a six-shooter cap gun
strapped to my hip,
I knew those bad guys
wouldn't give me no lip.
At the end of the day, with
the setting of the sun,
Mom called us all in, 'twas
the end of our fun.
But there was always tomorrow
when my stick horse and I
Would ride 'cross a prairie
under a blue western sky.
No fence could hold me; I
was free to run wild.
Oh, the wonderful imagination
I had as a child![1]

____

[1] Iowa Poetry Association winner first time
submission 2021.

When we are young, we spend so much time wishing we were older. And then when we grow old, we lament all the things that could have been and can be no more.

I'll be in the cold, cold ground one day.
But until that time, I'm just
tryin' to find my way.
Some days are sunny, and
the path is quite clear.
Other days are shrouded in fog—are
you there, Lord? Can you hear?
Then comes a voice so strong and clear,
"I'm right here beside you. I'm always near!"

It's those days when we're so tired and weary, and the end is creeping ever closer that I start to think of what lies ahead when this ole body is finally dead.

Soar, spirit, soar so I can finally be free—
Above the bondage of the earth,
where I can be just me.
Soar, spirit, soar to a land
where angels dwell—

Where all I'll feel is heaven's bliss
and know that all is well.
Soar, spirit, soar, don't let
man weep for me—
For I am happy and content
because I'm finally free!

Our Hectic Life

Have you had those days when you feel like your life is totally out of control? Family demands, work, committee meetings, household chores and repairs, sickness and doctor appointments, and more and more and more!

Clickety-clack, clickety-
clack, my life is like a
Runaway train on a track!
Faster and faster and faster it goes—
Years filled with laughter;
some filled with woe.
Clickety-clack, clickety-clack,
Must keep going forward,
can never turn back.
Up o'er the mountains and
down 'round the bend,
I'm riding this train to the bitter end!

Clickety-clack, clickety-clack,
My Lord and Savior promised
He'd someday be back.
Realms full of angels, family, and friends,
Waiting to greet me when
this earthly life ends!

It seems, the more we try to bring balance into our hectic lives, the more demands there are from all sides! I feel like a gymnast crossing a beam.

I inch my way across the narrow beam.
Family and friends pull from the left—
Obligations and commitments
pull from the right.
If either win, I lose—forever
Falling, falling into the abyss.
So I keep moving forward
day by day, by month,
By year, until I reach the end.
In triumph, with arms held high,
I leap in victory to my eternal end!

It's all any of us can do: just keep a positive attitude, keep the faith, and keep moving forward. Face your challenges as they come, and enjoy the good times, no matter how fleeting they sometimes feel.

As if we don't have enough drama and challenges in life, cancer and other dread diseases are the worst of all for the person suffering and for the loved ones standing helplessly by. I speak from personal experience after losing a sister, mother, and father to cancer and two other sisters and my daughter, who fought the battle and won, also myself. There used to be an old saying that what didn't kill you made you stronger. The person who said that must not have had a loved one die from cancer or had a personal catastrophic loss. Trials in life may or may not make you stronger, but there are days that treading water to keep from drowning in sorrow or pain is all a person can manage, let alone fighting it.

Sometimes I feel like a salmon
swimming upstream,
Grizzly claws slashing, eagle talons gashing,
Men trying to catch me as I make my run.
Sometimes I feel like a salmon
swimming upstream,

Headwaters gushing, always rushing
Toward my goal in waning sun.
Sometimes I feel like a salmon
swimming upstream,
Tired, teary, oh so weary.
Is my task on earth yet done?
Sometimes I feel like a salmon
swimming upstream.
Death's dark veil has now begun.
My job has ended as God intended,
Not death but life! I'm His chosen one!

The Clock

What was life like before we had clocks, watches, cell phones—so many things telling us the time—and knowing that time means schedules, deadlines, and expectations? Sometimes I feel that a clock is my enemy. Ever notice that a clock doesn't care what you have going on in your life? One night, in Yuma, Arizona—where my husband, Sam, and I used to winter—the ticking of the clock was so loud in the still desert night; it woke me. I was having trouble falling back to sleep. The more I tried to block it out, the louder the ticking seemed to get. I considered throwing something at it to knock it off the wall, then realized that I was the one being foolish, not that clock!

Tick, tock, tick, tock, my sole
purpose is to be a clock.
You wish my minutes and hours away
But I care not as I tick tock all day.
Worries and cares can't weigh me down.
It makes no difference if you smile or frown.
Because…*tick, tock, tick tock,*
I'm simply a clock!

PERSONALITY

Sam and I were what you would call a type A personality, while my darling daughter, Brandi, is a total type B. Type As are driven to succeed, demanding perfection from themselves and those around them. Bs, on the other hand, are mellow and prone to procrastination. In spite of it all, we have managed to survive each other and love each other dearly.

One year, while we were visiting her in Colorado, her soon-to-be ex-husband had once again hurt her feelings. I saw her making motions with her hands and saying softly to herself, "Think like a duck. Think like a duck." Wouldn't it be nice if our troubles could roll right off like water on a duck's back?

I wish I were a feathered duck—a
simple little quack.

All the rains of daily life would
roll right off my back!
While we all fight the battle of
pushing up the stream,
Ducks just merrily bob along,
so easy so it seems.
Have you ever seen a duck
have a silly marital spat?
No debts, no car troubles, no
arguing…can you imagine that?
Ducks can spend days swimming
and preening in the sun.
Humans have to go to work
from dawn 'til day is done.
Yes, I think I'd like to be a
shiny-feathered duck.
Unless, of course, my destiny was the
main dish at a church potluck!

❦

PTSD

At age seventy-eight, my husband, Sam, was diagnosed with post-traumatic stress disorder (PTSD), most likely a result of repressed memories from his time as a combat news photographer in Vietnam, a difficult and broken childhood, and other life stressors. Only people who live with someone with PTSD or a traumatic brain injury can understand how the nightmares, temper flares, and unreasonable expectations in daily life can understand that there are days when you feel like you're walking on eggshells.

> I tiptoe carefully, so
> very carefully across the
> eggshells, lest I awaken
> the angry beast. He awak-
> ens anyway with a roar of

15

disapproval and self-righteous indignation that I should be as impertinent as to enter his realm of perfection. I cringe and slowly, very slowly, tiptoe away…

It is difficult for the outside world to see what the struggles are as the person with PTSD can seem perfectly ordinary, even extraordinary, to those who aren't there from day to day.

A lone tear escaped and slid silently downward, giving no sign of the broken heart inside. "You're such a lucky woman," those who don't know declare. They don't see the hurtful looks or hear the threats and scorn because she is incapable of the perfection demanded by an imperfect person. And so, minute by minute, she waits for the latest storm to pass, knowing that if she can just make it through the next hour, the next day, life will continue on.

Just a few months ago, before Sam received help dealing with his disorder, he made the comment that he couldn't understand why I was tired and ready to hide away if only for a day. He said he married me because he knew I had broad shoulders and could manage anything that came my way. People with PTSD can be very critical, sometimes violent or aggressive. Sam wasn't violent, but he was sometimes critical and aggressive. Some people with PTSD are addicted to alcohol or drugs in an effort to dull the pain. All of this wears a loved one down with the weight of their own personal stress. Fortunately, because Sam had an alcoholic father, who became violent when he drank, Sam made an extra effort not to become that person.

I used to think I was Atlas, with broad shoulders to hold up all the trials of the world, but time has taken its toll, and those broad shoulders are now bent and tired. Some days, there is just too much to bear. Each harsh word and hard look send an arrow that pierces my heart. Someday I fear there will be nothing left inside, and I shall die. Until that day, the world and I continue on.

People with PTSD suffer from depression, but so do their caretakers! There are days when I felt my despair was even greater than his!

Falling…falling…falling
into a pit of despair,
Hoping someone will catch
me, but no one is there.

Darkness envelopes and becomes my tomb.
No light escapes into my
empty feelings of gloom.
Falling…falling…falling off
the face of the earth,
I've lost all joyful feelings—
no happiness, no mirth.
This veil of depression refuses to leave me…
I'm a small rubber raft on a storm-tossed sea.
I call for help, yet nobody hears…
And as the depression darkens,
then so do my fears.
Falling…falling…falling,
when will it ever end?
Shouldn't there be something better
waiting 'round the bend?

There are days when I let my mind wander to a safe place, where problems of daily life can't reach me.

There is a land far, far away, where
my mind can freely roam,
A land with no tears, a land with no fears,
Away from the bad days at home.

This land of mine brims with
sunshine—not showers.
There are waterfalls, green
meadows, and so many flowers.
When tempers flare, and life is unfair,
My mind takes me safely away
To this marvelous, make-believe land,
Where I can safely escape when I may.

DREAMS

Dreams. Did my mother have dreams when she married Dad in England during WWII? Did she have dreams of what her first unborn child would be? He died shortly after birth while my dad was still thousands of miles away at war. She was sitting in little Schaller, Iowa, with her in-laws, her own family still in England. Did she dream of what life would be like living in America after leaving war-torn Britain? Six children later, living in a too small house with too little money, did her dreams die? The one thing we weren't short of was love and care, but those are not always the things of dreams.

Run, run as fast as you can
into the arms of an imaginary man,
One who will hold you and treat you right.

He'll hug you and kiss you
and won't pick a fight!
Run, run as far as you can
Into a dream of your soap opera land—
Where men are handsome
and women sublime.
They have affairs and heartache
each day the same time!
Run, run, you must continue to run
To escape from a life that is no longer fun.
Daily cares now just weigh you down.
No matter what you do, it's
met with a frown.
So turn on your soaps, and dream a dream,
Temporarily forgetting how
your day has been.
Just let life's cares slowly melt away,
While you sit and watch
your soaps for the day.

LOVE

Love can be funny. Some of us meet that certain someone while still in childhood; and others must search a while and make a few mistakes along the way before the love of their life comes along. As of my writing this, Sam and I had been blessed with forty years together before he passed away. He was the love of my life. I discovered that long-lasting love is the best because you truly want and need each other, in spite of illnesses and flaws. He was fire, and I was too, two flames that when merged became fire all-consuming. Sometimes the blaze was torrid passion. Sometimes we were destroying everything with our hot-tempered flares—fire, the blessing and the curse that defined who we were. We were like moths drawn to our flames until death took your fire. Without you, my

own flame flickered until sometime death
will claim me also.

Isn't it funny when love is brand-new,
Your days fill with sunshine,
all bathed in warm hues?
Stolen kisses on a warm summer's day…
We were so young then, just lovers at play.
Your smile was like dawn
peeking over the rim.
The birds started singing; your
head started to swim!
And as the sun's rising burns
off morning dew,
So heats up your passion with
thoughts all askew.
Noon blazes hotly as love
reaches its prime…
Sultry and torrid and days oh sublime.
Then afternoon wanes, and
the cooling begins.
Instead of hot passion, the comfort sets in.
By sunset, you're quite the
most comical pair,
As a day's-end excitement is
your favorite old chair.

As days turn into weeks and then
months and then years,
Where did this simple longing go? Why
must we grow old?—I miss it so!
Stolen dreams snatched away from us all, as
Reality sets in like a funeral pall.
Experience love's offering,
both laughter and tears,
For you'll find all too soon that
the daylight will end,
As the light of your life
disappears 'round the bend.

LOVE AND HATE

It lies, lurking in the shadows, waiting to spring into our consciousness with all its ugliness and disdain. It feeds on hate—hate for our very being—because of the color of our skin.

One day, while my mother was still alive, we were having a conversation about one of the ladies in her five hundred card club with whom she was having some issues. I told her I personally really liked that particular person. With that, my mother quickly pointed out that my *problem* was that I liked everybody! Think how wonderful this world would be if we all truly did like everybody!

The civil war happened long, long ago.
So why do they continue to
hate each other so?

White against Black—Black against White
After all these years, they continue to fight!
God commanded us to "love our neighbor"
Not just our brother, sister,
father, and mother.
Your neighbor is all mankind—
Love them all, and soon you'll find
It makes no difference if you're
brown, black, or white
Simply love each other with all your might

COMING HOME

At age seventeen, when I graduated from Schaller High School, I could hardly wait to leave my small hometown for Sioux City. Through the years, I lived in South Dakota, Colorado, Hawaii, always swearing I would never go back to Iowa, where the summers are hot and miserable and winters equally so with cold and snow.

Then one year, something happened. Sam and I were tired of job stress, city-living stress, and the high cost of living. So where did we go?—to Iowa, close to family for me and a little closer for Sam as his family was all east of the Mississippi. Iowa is definitely easier on the budget, which allowed us to travel and spend winters in Arizona and definitely no traffic, no long lines. Turns out, Iowa

really is a beautiful state with much to offer.
I just had to "grow up" to appreciate it.

"Home is where the heart
is," so the saying goes,
Then my home is in Iowa,
with corn in tidy rows.
Iowa has retained its flavor of
rural, country charm;
You can leave your household doors
unlocked and leave without alarm.
Iowa folks are always there when
families are in dismay;
They'll harvest the beans, feed the
pigs, and bale the fields of hay.
The summers are hot and steamy;
winters are snowy and cold.
To live in such a crazy place, you
need a pioneer's spirit that's bold!
But when you look at the deep blue
skies, the lakes and fields and streams,
You can see why the people who settled
here discovered a lifelong dream;

Of living and dying, where life is
simpler than the city's hectic pace;
Where church is still an integral part;
families hold an honored place.
So no matter how far I travel,
many miles from here to there,
My home will always be Iowa—
in foul weather and in fair.

Of course, by late summer, when we've
made it through the heat and tornado season
of June and July, along comes August!

The green earth groans under the
weight of crops, not ready for harvest.
The fields and gardens of flowers
are at their peak of bloom…
Each trying to show that it is the best!
Days are humid—nights are too—
but even so I can't be blue!
The katydids are singing their
frantic mating song,
Knowing that all too soon,
autumn will be along!
So take a deep breath, as summer's
heady scents fill the air…

Perhaps spend some time at your
favorite county or state fair.
It's August in Iowa, and the earth is green,
With plenty of nature's beauty,
everywhere to be seen.

After decades of planning a four-lane
highway, stretching across Iowa, in the fall of
2018, that finally became a reality for those of
us living in the western side of the state. This is
a little ode to Highway 20:

I could have written a ditty about
a person, pet, or a city!
Instead I chose Highway 20, as it winds
through Iowa, a land of plenty.
From the bluffs of Dubuque and Mississippi
River across the plains and to the
Missouri, where the Loess Hills reign.
Just take your time, and you
will see so much more—
Rolling hills, deer, wild turkeys,
and other life galore.
The corn stands tall and gives
a wave as we drive by.

The soybeans sway in the breeze
and let out a peaceful sigh.
Each county has a large freedom rock,
painted in honor of those who serve.
And now Highway 20, across Iowa,
in its four-lane concrete bands,
Is a winding memorial of what man
can do with machine and hands.

SHOPPING

Shopping is in my genetic makeup. My mother loved to shop, as did her mother before her. I shopped with Sam, with my sisters, and with my friends when I was in Yuma during the winter. There's nothing like a good bargain or even the task of getting the weekly groceries done.

Shopping…shopping…I really love to shop!
Putting things in my shopping cart
makes such a nice kerflop!
I pick up a pretty blouse in a size
that's much too small—
I'm going to lose ten pounds
before next season after all.
I toss in a bunch of bananas
already way too ripe…

But I get them anyway 'cause
the price is really just right.
Next stop, housewares to
buy a new cake pan…
But somewhere along the way,
I get an electric fan.
Now on to purses…I'm going
to just take a look
But before I get halfway there,
I end up with a book!
I don't understand why my bank
balance is getting so low
'Til I realize, all this shopping
has dealt my budget a blow!

ALZHEIMER'S

There are no good diseases, but one of the cruelest has to be Alzheimer's. The person, at first, realizes that they are slowly fading away—losing everything that makes them who they are. And for the loved ones standing by, how terribly sad as the person forgets who they are and, finally, sometimes after years of suffering, simply fade away until death brings them mercy and peace. In the last few months of his life, Sam had dementia caused by his failing kidneys and accelerated by dialysis.

> Like a troublesome gnat, he
> kept coming back!
> She'd chase him away; he'd
> be there the next day!

"Please don't bother me, don't
do me any harm!"
The look on his face was filled with alarm…
"Remember me? I live here too!
I've been married for forty
years only to you!"
Then a smile came across her face.
She looked at him in brief
recognition—the tiniest trace.
Then that mind-robbing
disease swiftly returned
As she cried in alarm, "Please don't
bother me, don't do me any harm!"

THE BUG

It all started when my sister, Janet, bought a VW Bug. Then my niece, Allyson, bought hers. I knew then that I wanted my own little VW Bug, and so the quest began. A couple of months later, Daisy came into my life. I loved that little Beetle Bug, even though it needed a number of costly repairs in the first few months I owned her. I had never had a six-speed car before. The first time I kicked it into turbo gear, there was a thrill I hadn't felt since my teen years in my '56 Chevy.

> Cruising down the highway—
> my VW Bug and I,
> Listening to some Beach Boys'
> tunes, I feel like I could fly!
> First gear, second gear, third,
> fourth, and fifth—

If you think a Bug is slow,
you're believing in a myth!
I slip it into sixth gear—that's
turbo speed, you know.
My Bug and I are zinging by
cars and trucks so slow.
Until I glimpse in the mirror at those
awful flashing red and blue lights—
Ole Smokey Bear has gotten me
in his radar speed gun's sights!
After I pull my Bug unto the
shoulder of Interstate 29,
As ole Smokey hands me that slip of
paper, I know I'm getting a fine!
My Bug and I are grounded;
now I tell you with a sigh…
But for one brief moment on a
summer's day, I felt that I could fly!

THE LAST GOODBYE

Humans have fought and killed other humans since the beginning of time. Each war takes its toll, not only in the total destruction of property and life but in the after-effects on the survivors. Husbands or wives left without a partner, children without their parents. Yet we continue to fight and continue to say goodbye yet again.

This could be our last chance to
tell each other goodbye—
To say the words "I love you"
and the reasons why.
This could be the last time we
get to say goodbye—
One last hug, one last kiss, it
makes me want to cry!

Why must man go to war,
leaving loved ones behind?
Family and friends, who are left to
grieve—Lord, please give me a sign!
Land is gained. Land is lost—
all at one tremendous cost.
And yet we survive…
In spite of it all, we continue to thrive.
But this could be our last chance
to tell each other goodbye…
I dread that call to tell me that
you are gone and died.

THE DREAM

As a Christian, I know I am not supposed to worry. As a human, however, that ole worry bug sometimes attacks but not as badly as it used to before I had the dream…

> My large suitcase and two other bags seemed heavier than ever after an exhausting journey.
> As I stood there in the terminal, wondering how I was going to manage, a gentleman offered to carry the cumbersome suitcase for me. Usually, I would be leery of handing over a suitcase to a stranger, but there was

something kind and trustworthy about him, so I agreed.

We hadn't gone far when he could see I was struggling with the other two bags and told me to give him another one. I protested. (After all, he was already carrying the largest one. And how could I expect him to carry so much of my load?) He made a motion with his hand to put the second bag onto it, and so I reluctantly agreed. He went ahead without a word.

The final bag was dingy, with sisal rope handles. How had I ever let myself get burdened with such an ugly, embarrassing, and heavy load! He spoke my name then and commanded me to give him the third bag. This time, I protested loudly. After all, the bags were mine. How could I expect this kind stranger to carry it all, especially that horrible final bag? But for some reason, as I struggled to carry it myself, it became heavier and more difficult with every step. I finally relented and handed that dingy, dull bag of trouble over.

I awoke with a start! It had been a dream! But as I came out of the twilight of sleep, a very gentle voice spoke to me, not the kind of voice you hear out loud but distinct and loud without speaking. The voice said, "I am the Lord. I was sent here to carry your burdens." Tears formed in my eyes, and for several days after that, every time I thought about the voice and that dream, I cried, not with fear but with joy. For that dream, and the voice that followed showed me that, even though there were problems in my life, Jesus was there to carry the heavy load.

That ugly bag with sisal rope handles stood for all the things that were weighing me down—everyday things that momentarily make me lose sight of the one who was sent to help in time of need. Now, when I feel problems are over-whelming, and I'm too tired to cope, I call to the Lord and ask Him to

please carry yet another
piece of baggage. I, at
once, start to feel a light-
ness as He lifts away the
load. As stated in Isaiah
53:4, "Surely he has
borne our griefs and car-
ried our sorrows."

I stood there in the terminal,
suitcase by my side,
When suddenly, from nowhere,
a voice to me did cry.
"Let me carry that suitcase
and the heavy other two.
I came so you won't be burdened
by things that make you blue."
I readily relinquished the
biggest case with ease,
And then, with just a little thought,
gave another to appease.
But then the stranger told me,
"Give me that last one too."
But stubbornly, I held on to that
bag, as if the thing were glued.

He said that He would carry
everything I had instead,
That I didn't have to do this alone;
because for this, He'd bled.
You see, that baggage is my life,
my sorrows, and my fears.
The man who kindly took them was
Christ, my Savior, who wipes away all tears.
Now I see Him as the one
who carries all my woes,
That I don't have to do it alone,
that he is there wherever I go.
As I travel down life's long and lonely trail,
I call on Him, who was the porter
of my baggage of travail.
And just like the story of the
footprints in the sand,
He'll carry my baggage and me
'til I'm in the heavenly land.

REGRETS

I took a long hiatus from writing to care for my beloved Sam. Facing the loss is still difficult, and there are days when I am lost without him, floating somewhere between reality and dreams of our forty years together.

On August 22, 2021, Sam passed away at age eighty-three from cystic kidney disease. Dialysis worked for a while…until it didn't. He was too old for a transplant, and so I watched this brilliant, creative light of my life slowly fade into nothing but a shell. When I told him I loved him forever, and I knew he loved me too, that it was okay to let go and join the rest of his loved ones in heaven, I couldn't fathom how permanent his departure was really going to be. Oh, I had planned financially. Sam's obituary was written and his will up to date, but the impact of never feeling him next to me, never getting to kiss his lips, or hold his hand again has left me with this giant hole in my heart.

Like a moth to flame, you lured me in,
Smoldering brown eyes that
set my heart on fire.
You burned your way into my
every thought and feeling…
Twenty-four hours a day, I was
obsessed by your smile, your
touch, and being close to you.
Your very kiss ignited a fever that
only having you would quench and
then reignite all over again.
When you died, my fire went
with you to the grave.
My days are dark without you by my side…
Like a never-ending winter.

Regrets—we all have them. There are regrets over things we did or didn't do when opportunities arose, regrets over words spoken or left unsaid. The longer we live, the more regrets we amass if we let ourselves.

Coulda, woulda, should have
done...all remorseful laments.
If I, wish I, why didn't I do...
it really doesn't make sense!
We mourn the minutes and hours gone
by for which nothing can be done,
Instead of being thankful for the
present days as they come!
As quickly as a tick becomes tock,
time continues to march along.
There isn't anything man can do
to change this age-old song.
Of present and future becoming the
past, it happens for me and you,
So why not resolve to let it pass
without those "if only I'd" blues!
The future is uncertain; the
past we can't undo.
And so today is all we have, so live
life through and through.

Another regret was for my daughter. I regret that she had to go through such heartbreak after losing her husband to her best friend and her job all within a few months' period of time. There were more losses after that, major ones. Even though she lost much through the years that were dear to her, she refused to give up on life, even after surviving ovarian cancer the year after Sam died, so this poem is dedicated to her.

After you left me, sunny days
turned into dreary nights
As I tossed on a bed of tears and fright.
After you left me, symphonies
ceased to play—
Children's laughter fell on
deaf ears as I blindly
Struggled to make it through each day.
After you left me, it took a very long time
For me to realize that there
was a "me" after "you."
And slowly…slowly the sun began to shine.

ODDS 'N' ENDS

Who will kill the spiders now
that you are gone?
I counted on you for many years
to set the insect bombs!
And who will catch the little mice
that come into my house?
I know that you're in heaven now,
so I really hate to grouse!
Your leaving here has really
dealt me quite a blow.
Who will shovel all that drifting,
blowing winter snow?
I really think it's quite unfair
you've left me by myself.
Now all I have are memories
and your photos on a shelf.

*****

My shadow friend is with
me everywhere I go—
Whether in the darkness of the
night or daytime's sunny glow!

*****

The musical laugh of a child at play can
bring sunshine and joy to a dreary day!
Birds that sing, furry puppies, and kittens
Bring warmth to your heart,
like a soft pair of mittens!
Sunshine and rainy days
and flowers in bloom
Can bring on a smile that
would fill up a room.
Just look around you, dear
friend, and then you'll see,
There's a joyous world waiting
for you and me!

*****

Ragtime, Charleston…years ago gone by,
But the soulful song of the
cowboy, never will it die.

For the cowboy sings from within his heart
Of cattle, land, and earthly
things of which he's a part.
A cowboy croons of lost loves, cryin'
in his beer…of honky-tonks and
Lonesome nights and wishin' she was near.
The years may come; the years may go.
But really, don't you know?
The cowboy's song will never
die; it's life itself—his soul.

*****

Years come, years go…sometimes way
too fast and others way too slow!
If I don't feel sorry for myself, who will?
Family members and friends all have
challenges of their own. So…I will throw
a party for one and invite myself to have
a pity party just for me!

*****

I try to hide——to make myself
very small and invisible.

Then the world finds me again
as reality rears its ugly head.
If I am very quiet, perhaps life's ugliness
won't notice me, and I can breathe
a sigh of relief as it slips not so silently by.
In my youth, I stepped forward with my
chest puffed out, ready to take on the world.
Now I'm older, wiser, and tired, so the
battle is no longer important… just
surviving each day becomes a priority.
The sun rises. The sun sets.
Babies are born. People die. And I'm
here as a witness to it all…a time of
rejoicing but, more often, a time of
mourning as I say goodbye yet again.
I hate this process of growing old. The poet,
Robert Browning, had it wrong when he
said, "Grow old along with me! The best
is yet to be." The best has already been…

*****

(To the tune of "Bye, Bye, Blackbird")
Pack up all your cares and woes;
on the Lord there they go.
Bye, bye, worries.

Won't be coming back, you see,
He is looking after me.
Bye, bye, worries.
Fill your life with joy and
love and giving and in
The Lord you'll find such peaceful living.
Pack up all your cares and woes;
on the Lord there they go—
Worries, bye, bye…worries, bye, bye!

*****

Summer lets out a heavy sigh of relief as autumn breezes rustle through the trees to announce its arrival.

*****

Why is it that the smallest things in life bother us the most? Like a gnat buzzing around our eyes and nose with great persistence; all those little problems in life plague us.

*****

As I gaze into the pool of life, there
is no sorrow, anger, strife.
All I see reflecting back as me are things
wonderful there can possibly be.
I see blue skies and rainbows
and couples in love,
Puppies and kittens and soft cooing doves.
The pool of life is your inside out, a true
reflection of what your life is about.
Some people see fighting
and sadness and wars,
Arguing, divorces, and slamming of doors!
Others see daisies and roses
and poppies in bloom
No clouds overshadow, no
dark pending doom.
So look hard into YOUR pool of life.
Make sure you reflect only
goodness most rife.

*****

It all began one day when
Georgie stubbed his toe...
He jumped around and cussed
and let out such a yell,

unto the pavement, poor old Georgie fell!
No sooner, a scream passed through his lips,
Then Georgie found he'd broken both hips!
Luckily, a man who was passing by
heard him, as in pain he cried.
But before the ambulance came,
The heavens opened up,
and it began to rain!
Georgie forgot all about his toe 'cause after
all that grief, he died, ya know!

*****

It was that moment in time
we used to dread,
When Mom or Dad would announce
it was already time for bed.
It made no difference if we
were watching a show.
What Mom and Dad said, in those
days, was always law, you know.

And so with long faces, we'd
climb up the stairs,
Dragging along our favorite
dolly or ragged teddy bears.

*****

I've been here before, struggling
with this door.
Should I stay safely behind it or risk
going out into a world unfit?
If I stay, perhaps I can be safely hidden away,
For if I go, there is a world riddled
so full of crime and woe.

*****

A folded flag, a casket lowered into the grave
Silent tears for the life they gave.
Air force, army, navy, marines,
and coast guard too,
Men and women of valor
who sacrificed for you.

*****

58

This is a quote from Dr. Seuss: "Don't cry because it's over. Smile because it happened."

*****

I have this little ditty that's
stuck inside my head.
It repeats itself all day long and
worse when I'm in bed!
I've tried to drown it out with
a hearty glass of wine.
But instead of blotting out that tune,
I'm tapping my foot in time!
Two more glasses of wine should
certainly do the trick.
But instead of drowning out the
tune, I find myself quite sick!
And as for that ditty going around my head
The wine finally worked because now
my head is throbbing instead!

*****

Hickory, dickory dock, I keep
looking at the clock!
The days go so slow 'cause of
COVID, you know!
Hickory, dickory dock.

*****

She'd run with all her might…that
skinny little child trying to beat a
shadow cast down by a cloud.
As she grew older, the race continued. But
instead of a shadow from a cloud, she
raced to excel…to stand out in the crowd.
As years went by, she realized she longed
for those early times when that skinny
little girl would spend her days
racing the shadows of a cloud.

*****

I loved you; you loved me. We
were as happy as we could be!
Laughter and tears, trials and fears,
together we made it through many years.

I loved you; you loved me until God
decided to take you away from me.

*****

Round and round
Up and down
Life's carousel

About the Author

Ann Sears is a retiree, whose career included many different hats. She was an executive secretary by trade; but moving to different states and cities taught her to diversify, including working in a newspaper production layout, writing radio commercials, and being a real estate broker and relocation director, to name a few. Each change brought new life experiences. Ann has Christian values that guide her in daily life and challenges. In her spare time, she enjoys quilting for charities with a group of fellow Christian women, knitting hats for the needy, spending time with family, or relaxing to a variety of music, especially jazz.

www.ingramcontent.com/pod-product-compliance
Lightning Source LLC
Chambersburg PA
CBHW022102150726
47990CB00003B/1205